Doctrinal Teaching Statement of Valley Bible Church

Approved by the Valley Bible Church Elder Board – 08/19/2013
Revision 1 – 10/12/13
Revision 2 – 09/08/21

Preface

We become what we think and what we think comes from words. For Christians, this means God's words, as they are recorded in Scripture, must be of primary importance to us. This document contains the Doctrinal Teaching Statement of Valley Bible Church of Hercules, California. It is a summary of the words that form the doctrines and practices that we teach. We believe that they are foundational in understanding God's revelation to us, the Bible, and what God expects of us. We believe that some of these doctrines or practices seem to have been ignored or discarded by some of the modern evangelical church. When this happens, false teaching of all kinds can fill the void resulting in a false gospel that seduces people into thinking they are saved when they are not. In turn, this results in the church being merely a crowd gathering for some kind of religious experience.

This Doctrinal Teaching Statement is intentionally not identical to the Valley Bible Church's Doctrinal Statement, as presented in our Constitution and Bylaws or our Statement of Faith as found on our Website. The Doctrinal Statement in the constitution represents the minimum doctrinal standard for membership in our church. The Doctrinal Teaching Statement goes beyond the Doctrinal Statement by presenting a much fuller explanation of the doctrines we hold dear. We use this more detailed Doctrinal Teaching Statement as the standard for what is taught at Valley Bible Church. With respect to the Doctrinal Statement, we want to be both Biblically accurate as well as gracious and inclusive as we can be in welcoming all who embrace the primary or essential doctrines of the Christian faith, even though there may be differing opinions on various secondary issues or doctrines. The Doctrinal Teaching Statement, however, allows us to remain fully faithful in consistently teaching the whole counsel of God as we believe it is revealed in Scripture. So it is with a love for God and His people and a commitment to eternal truth that we offer and require this Doctrinal Teaching Statement to be the standard for all adult teachers and teaching at Valley Bible Church.

Table of Contents

ARTICLE ONE
Scripture

We believe the Scriptures teach that the sixty-six books of the Bible are God's only propositional revelation to man (Deuteronomy 4:2; 1 Corinthians 2:13; 1 Thessalonians 2:13; Revelation 22:18-19). All sixty-six books are God-breathed, without error in part or the whole, with every word verbally inspired by God, inerrant in the original documents, and the only sufficient and infallible rule for life and practice (Matthew 5:18; John 17:17; 1 Corinthians 2:13; 2 Timothy 3:15-17). The truths in the Bible are objective propositions God wants man to know, written through the supervision of the Holy Spirit utilizing the individual styles of human authors as they composed and recorded God's Word to man (1 Corinthians 2:13; 1 Thessalonians 2:13; 2 Peter 1:20-21). While there are many applications of Scripture, there is only one intended interpretation. The grammatical-historical method of interpretation of Scripture is the best way to determine the most literal, normal meaning of the words in Scripture, under the illumination of the Holy Spirit (John 16:13; 1 Corinthians 2:10-16). The Bible contains all the words that God intended for His people to have at all stages in history, including today. Though Satan has blinded the mind of the unbeliever from understanding spiritual truth (1 Corinthians 2:14; 2 Corinthians 4:4), the Bible is completely sufficient to tell believers everything they need to know about salvation and how to grow in sanctification (2 Timothy 3:16-17; Hebrews 4:12), both in the personal life of the believer and in the corporate life of the church. The Bible is authoritative for all matters of life, faith and practice and it is the final authoritative word for the church and for all matters on which it speaks.

We deny that truth is merely a social construct or that truth can be grounded in anything other than the veracity of Scripture and the propositions it asserts. We deny that the Bible contains any error in the original writings or that any part can be set against any other part. We deny any additional authoritative revelation of spiritual truth received outside of the Bible from all other religious writings, papal decrees, dreams, "prophetic utterances," or ideas.

ARTICLE TWO
God

We believe the Scriptures teach that there is only one God (Deuteronomy 6:4; Joshua 22:22; 1 Corinthians 8:4; James 2:19), and all things were created by Him, and for Him, and through Him in six consecutive twenty-four-hour days (Exodus 20:11; Psalm 33:6; Romans 11:36). He is One in essence, yet eternally exists in three Persons, the Father, Son, and Holy Spirit (Matthew 28:19-20; Luke 3:22; John 14:16, 26; Galatians 4:6). He is an infinite, all-knowing being, perfect in all His attributes and actions, and has no limitations inconsistent with His nature (Job 11:7-9). By His universal and timeless decree, He orders and governs all things, from the immense galaxies of space to sub-atomic particles, according to His purpose, will, and time (Isaiah 46:7-11). He alone is completely sovereign and asserts His divine will over all creation (Psalm 99:1), international and national authorities (Daniel 2:21; 4:4-37; Isaiah 10:13), individual lives (2 Samuel 1:6-7; Psalm 75:6-7), the will of man (Exodus 12:35-36; 1 Samuel 24:10, 18), "random" occurrences in life (Proverbs 16:33), the exercise of sin (Genesis 20:6; 50:20), and the election of His own in salvation (Ephesians 1:4-5). We deny that God is divided in any way.

We deny that He is limited in any of His attributes or perfections, or that He grows in knowledge or power, reacting to the will and actions of man. We deny that He is the author of sin or that His work of grace abrogates the accountability of man for his sin. We deny that He is Father of all men, having adopted only those who come to Him through Jesus Christ as His sons.

ARTICLE THREE
The Father

We believe the Scriptures teach that the Father is God (Ephesians 4:6; Romans 15:6; 1 Corinthians 15:24; John 6:27). God the Father is the ultimate source of all things (1 Corinthians 8:6). Scripture teaches that the Father and the Son are equal in nature and even though equal the Son would assume a role of subordination to the Father in the execution of divine purposes (John 1:1, 2). He also has a Fatherhood relationship to spirit beings, thus expressing His authoritative headship (Job 1:6; Heb.12:9). By means of the grace of God and the atoning work of the Son on the cross, He now forgives the sins of those who put their faith in Christ and thus enters a Fatherhood relationship with them through their spiritual birth, by which He indwells them, thus making them partakers of the divine nature, and calling them His born ones (1 John 3:9; Eph. 4:6; 2 Peter 1:4) and adopts them as His own sons through Christ (Eph. 1:5). The Father is the One who sent the Son as His gift into the world (John 3:16). Moreover, He, in partnership with the Son, sent the Holy Spirit to be resident in the world on the Day of Pentecost (John 14:26; 15:26).

ARTICLE FOUR
Jesus Christ

We believe the Scriptures teach that Jesus Christ is fully God and fully man, in undiluted and perfect union as the Second Person of the Trinity, possessing all the divine attributes of God (John 10:30; 14:9). Though eternally co-existing with God the Father before, during, and after the Incarnation (John 1:1; Philippians 2:6-7), He was conceived by the Holy Spirit, born of the virgin Mary (Matthew 1:23), laid aside His privileges as God, and took on the limitations of a human body at the Incarnation (Philippians 2:6-7) in order to demonstrate the great love of the Father (1 John 4:10), justify the believing sinner before God (Romans 3:24-25; 2 Corinthians 5:21), remove the penalty and power of sin from believers (1 Peter 2:24), and establish His right to rule over God's Kingdom (Isaiah 9:6; Matthew 1:23; John 1:1; Philippians 2:6-11; Colossians 2:9). Though sinless, and incapable of sinning (Matthew 4:1; Hebrews 13:8; James 1:13), Jesus experienced every kind of temptation man faces (Hebrews 4:15). His death on the cross was voluntary, vicarious, substitutionary, propitiatory, and redemptive in God's sight (John 10:17; Romans 3:24-25). The death, burial, and bodily resurrection of Jesus Christ is essential to the gospel and guarantees the future resurrection of all believers to eternal life (Romans 10:9-10; 1 Corinthians 15:17, 20). Following His physical resurrection, He ascended to heaven where He serves as the believer's Intercessor, Advocate and the Head of His church (Romans 8:34; Ephesians 5:23; 1 John 2:1). He will bring recorded history to an end through the rapture of His church, His millennial rule on earth, and His eternal rule in the new heaven and new earth (1 Thessalonians 4:13-18; Revelation 20:6; 22:5).

We deny that Jesus was a created being. We deny that he is not a member of the Trinity, or merely a good moral example, or simply a human prophet or teacher. We deny that He was a "spirit brother" to Lucifer, or that He was only a man who received a divine "gnosis" when He was on the cross.

ARTICLE FIVE
The Holy Spirit

We believe the Scriptures teach that the Holy Spirit is the Third Person of the Trinity, co-equal in essence and deity with the Father and the Son, and is Himself called God (Acts 5:3-4; 1 Corinthians 3:16). He was active in creation (Genesis 1:2), the Incarnation of Christ (Matthew 1:18), the written revelation of Scripture (2 Peter 1:20-21), and continues to be active in the work of salvation (John 3:5-7). Though active in the Old Testament in the empowering of leaders (Numbers 11:17), preaching (1 Samuel 10:10), comfort (Psalm 51:10), and revelation (Ezekiel 8:3), the work of the Holy Spirit in the church began at the first post-resurrection Pentecost, when He visited the early apostles and others with visible signs of power (Acts 2:3-4), and began the work of building the Church through bringing conviction of sin (1 Corinthians 14:24), imputing righteousness to believers (2 Corinthians 5:21), and transforming believers into the image of Christ (2 Corinthians 3:18). He is clearly seen to be a person and part of the Trinity by His intelligence (Romans 8:16), will (Acts 16:7; 1 Corinthians 12:11), and affections (Isaiah 63:10; Ephesians 4:30). He indwells all believers at the time of salvation (1 Corinthians 12:13), making their bodies His temple (1 Corinthians 3:16; 2 Corinthians 6:16). Believers are to seek continuous filling (control) by the Holy Spirit resulting in Spirit-filled worship, thanks, and relationships (Ephesians 5:18-33). The Holy Spirit is the sole agent of regeneration (John 3:5-6), baptizes believers into the body of Christ (1 Corinthians 12:13), seals them for heaven (Ephesians 1:13), indwells them (1 Corinthians 6:19), fills them (Ephesians 5:18), and assures them of their salvation (Romans 8:16). The Holy Spirit guides believers into the truth (John 14:16; 16:13), dispenses spiritual gifts (1 Corinthians 12:7), teaches them all things (Luke 12:12; John 14:26), comforts them (2 Corinthians 1:4), brings conviction (John 16:8), reveals God's truths through Scripture (1 Corinthians 2:10-14), and intercedes for them (Romans 8:26-27).

5.1 Spiritual Gifts – We believe the Scriptures teach that there are a variety of spiritual gifts listed in the New Testament. Their primary purpose is the edification and equipping of the body and they include serving, giving, mercy, exhortation, teaching, evangelism, leadership, and others (Romans 12:6-8; Ephesians 4:11-12; 1 Corinthians 12:7-10). We also teach that several of the gifts mentioned in the above passages, specifically tongues (known languages), healing, apostleship, and others, were specifically given to reveal and authenticate the message and ministry of the apostles (Acts 2:22, 2 Corinthians 12:12; Hebrews 2:4.) With the canon of the New Testament complete, these "sign gifts" are no longer needed. The evidence of the New Testament and two thousand years of history does not reveal the ongoing nature of these gifts. Therefore, we believe the Scriptures teach that the gifts of tongues, interpretation, healing, and miracles are not the norm for usage in the church today.

We deny that the Holy Spirit is merely a "force" and not a person of the Trinity. We deny the existence of a second "baptism" of the Holy Spirit after salvation. We deny that the "sign" gifts are the norm for the church today. We deny that the Holy Spirit adds to the revelation of Scripture by speaking in tongues, visions, dreams, and speaking to people today, other than through the affirmation of Scripture.

ARTICLE SIX
Man

We believe the Scriptures teach that man was created in the image of God, free of sin in all his faculties, with no immorality in him (Genesis 1:26-27). Man was created to enjoy fellowship with God and to glorify Him (Romans 11:36; Colossians 1:16; Revelation 5:12), but lost that privilege and his innocence in the sin of Adam. Adam acted as the federal head of the race and when he sinned, all mankind fell spiritually with him (Genesis 3:17-24; Romans 5:12-21), resulting in spiritual and physical death, and complete estrangement from God (Genesis 2:17; 3:19). Man today still bears the scars of Adam's sins. He is estranged from God from his birth (Psalm 51:5), born physically alive but spiritually dead (Ephesians 2:1), manifesting hostility to God, being unable and unwilling to respond to God (Romans 8:7). By his inherited nature and his own actions, he is helpless and hopeless, (Jeremiah 17:9; Romans 1:18-20; 3:9-20), showing himself to be evil, spiritually ignorant, rebellious, wayward, and useless to God (Romans 3:10-18). He is neither worthy of being saved nor does he want to be. And yet God will hold him accountable for his own actions. He is given the truth of God in creation (Romans 1:19-20) and the conviction of his own conscience (Romans 2:15). But in suppressing this truth (Romans 1:18), he is held responsible for it and will be left without excuse (Romans 1:20).

We deny that man's basic problem is the place where he was born, his family heritage, a tattered self-image, lack of education, his environment, his social status, or his financial means. We deny that there is any type of "prevenient grace" dwelling in man that makes him able to seek and secure salvation on his own. We deny that man can choose to be saved, since his conversion comes through repentance and faith, which are gifts from God.

ARTICLE SEVEN
Sin

We believe the Scriptures teach that sin originated in the angelic world with Satan (Isaiah 14:12-14; John 8:44; 2 Peter 2:4), and was extended to man through the rebellious choice of Adam (Romans 5:12), resulting in a universal sin nature for all mankind (Ephesians 2:1-3). Sin is an inner presence in every human being that compels attitudes and actions that are hostile to God (Romans 3:9-11; 8:7). Sin is further described as moral transgression (Romans 4:15), missing the mark of God's standard (Romans 3:9; 5:12), moral lapses, faults, or mistakes (Galatians 6:1), spiritual indebtedness (Matthew 6:12; Romans 4:4), lawlessness (1 John 3:4), and failure to do what one knows is right (James 4:17). Man's intellect (2 Corinthians 4:4), conscience (Romans 2:15), will (Romans 1:28), and heart (Ephesians 4:18) are all affected by sin, yielding him completely unable and unwilling to respond to God in a positive manner (Romans 8:7-8; Ephesians 2:1-3). This does not mean that man is as morally depraved as he could be, or that he will indulge in every form of sin possible. But it does mean that corruption extends to every part of his being, leaving him with no spiritual virtue or power (Romans 7:18; Ephesians 4:18; Titus 1:15). Man is an absolute slave to his sin nature (John 8:34), being unable to change his fundamental preference for sin and self to love God in any consequential way, or to do any act that would answer to the demands of God's holy law (John 15:4-5; 1 Corinthians 2:14). Even one sin makes him guilty of the whole law (James 2:10). The penalty of sin is death (Romans 5:12-14; 6:23; James 1:15). Without God's intervention to save him, man is doomed to eternal separation from God in the bottomless pit of hell (Revelation 14:11; 20:15), sealed by God's eternal judgment at the Great White Throne Judgment (Revelation 20:11-15).

We deny that sin is man's broken self-image or that someone else is responsible for his sin. We deny that man's sin is a result of his environment, socio-economic status, family background or lack of education. We deny that sin is not spiritually fatal. We deny that God is the author of sin.

ARTICLE EIGHT
Salvation

8.1 The Means – We believe the Scriptures teach that salvation is wholly a work of the grace of God, accomplished on the basis of Christ's life and completed work on the cross, and is not the result of man's will, merit, or work (John 1:7-8; Ephesians 2:8-10; 1 Peter 1:18-19). We believe the Scriptures teach that there is "no other name under heaven" that can save mankind other than the name of Jesus Christ (Acts 4:12). Since the Scriptures also leave no doubt as to the need for salvation (John 3:3, 5, 7; 1 Corinthians 2:14), Jesus Christ comes as the only answer to man's dilemma, the only one who can mediate between God and man and pay for man's sins (1 Timothy 2:5). As the Forgiver of sins (Acts 5:31; 10:43; 1 John 3:5) and the Giver of life (John 10:10), Jesus Christ is the sole Savior of man (John 14:6; Acts 4:12).

We deny that salvation comes through anything other than God's grace. We deny that man is saved through the intervention or means of any church, teaching of man, good work, sincere faith in any other religion, social action, or the impetus to love.

8.2 Election – We believe the Scriptures teach that God chose the elect for salvation before the foundation of the world (Matthew 25:34; Ephesians 1:4; 2 Thessalonians 2:13; 2 Timothy 1:9). This is the act of the Father giving repentant sinners to Jesus, resulting in belief, obedience, and eternal salvation (John 17:6-10). This is absolutely necessary, given the condition of man as explained in Article Six (Man) and Article Seven (Sin). Election is often paired with foreknowledge (Jeremiah 1:5; Romans 8:29), indicating God's predetermined intimate knowledge of those He would save, not His knowledge of those who would respond to Him in the future (Matthew 7:23; Acts 2:23; Romans 8:29). This would make man the initiator of his own salvation and God responding to the faith of man. Instead, Scripture teaches that salvation is not the result of man's will, but an act of God's sovereign will alone (John 1:13; Romans 9:11-13; 2 Timothy 1:9). Only God can draw man to salvation; and His call to the elect is certain and effective (John 6:37, 39, 44, 65; Ephesians 2:5-6). God's call becomes effective when man hears the gospel (Romans 10:14), and God lifts the veil of spiritual blindness (2 Corinthians 4:4), opens the heart of the sinner (Acts 16:14), gives the gift of faith (Acts 15:9; Galatians 3:22; Ephesians 2:8-9; Philippians 1:29), and leads the sinner to repent through His kindness (Romans 2:4). God does not elect anyone for damnation (Romans 9:22; James 1:13; 2 Peter 3:9), nor does election negate man's responsibility to respond to God. Every unsaved person will someday stand before God and be judged (Hebrews 9:27; Revelation 20:12), not by whether or not he rejected the gospel, but because he suppressed the truth that God gave him (Romans 1:18-20, 26-32; 2:14-16), he loved the darkness of his unbelief and evil deeds (John 3:19), he hardened his heart (Hebrews 4:7), he chose to obey unrighteousness, wrath and indignation (Romans 2:8), and thus deserves God's judgment because of his sin (Romans 6:23, Galatians 6:7-8). Man is saved by God's grace and damned by his own sin and works. Ultimately, this is a mystery to him because he cannot understand how God seemingly ordains everything according to His will, which includes the ordaining of the voluntary choices of moral creatures. We also teach that children who are not old enough to suppress the truth of God and reject Him (Romans 1:18), and those who have never had the mental capability to perceive right and wrong are also chosen by God for salvation (Deuteronomy 1:39; 1 Kings 14:13), and we will see them again in heaven (2 Samuel 12:22-23).

We deny that election is based on foreknowledge of man's response or that it only means election to good works. We also deny that the Bible teaches double predestination or reprobation. We deny that man is the initiator in his own salvation or that he can choose to be saved apart from the work of the Holy Spirit. We deny that man can repent, have faith, believe, or confess on his own. We deny that man has a spark of grace or faith within him, since this is impossible for one who is spiritually dead.

8.3 Regeneration – We believe the Scriptures teach that one must be spiritually born again in order to see the kingdom of God (John 3:3, 7). Regeneration is an act of God without any merit on the part of the recipient (Titus 3:5). In accordance with His elective will and perfect timing (Ephesians 1:11; Titus 1:3), He ensures that the gospel is brought to the elect through the faithful efforts of those already saved (Acts 15:7; Romans 10:14), lifts the veil from the eyes of the spiritually dead (1 Corinthians 2:14; 2 Corinthians 4:4), provides the gifts of faith and repentance (Acts 11:18; Ephesians 2:8-9), causes the elect to listen and believe the gospel (Ephesians 1:11-13), baptizes them into His body through the power of the Holy Spirit (1 Corinthians 12:13), adopts them as sons and daughters (Romans 8:15; Ephesians 1:5), and seals them for eternity to the praise of His glory (Ephesians 1:13-14). Even though the repentant sinner may not know exactly when this happens, it is an instantaneous act of the Holy Spirit brought about through hearing the Word of God and believing in Christ (John 5:24). Genuine salvation is seen by complete turning from sin in repentance (Acts 2:38), a belief in, and confession of, the person and completed work of Christ on the cross (Romans 10:9-10), a hunger and thirst for righteousness (Matthew 5:6), devotion to Christ alone above all other people and things (Matthew 10:37; Mark 10:21; Luke 9:23), spiritual fruit that is consistent with repentance (Galatians 5:22-23), a desire to know God's Word (1 Peter 2:2), love for, and participation in, the life of the church (Hebrews 10:24-25; 1 John 2:9-11), the exercise of spiritual gifts (Ephesians 4:11-12; 1 Peter 4:10), good works (Ephesians 2:10), and faithful service to God (Ephesians 4:12).

We deny that regeneration occurs because of evangelistic appeals, persuasive speech, emotional responses, verbal profession, faith in faith, or spiritual works. We also deny that regeneration takes place through a change of mind, joining a church, moral reformation, "turning over a new leaf," or man's decision.

8.4 The Gospel – We believe the Scriptures teach that the elect come to salvation through the proclamation and apprehension of the gospel, which literally means "good news." This refers to the good news of God reaching out to man through the death, burial, and resurrection of Jesus Christ in order to make provision for the sin of all who would believe and come to Him (John 6:37; 17:8). The one who receives the gospel understands that he is a sinner, hopelessly devoid of any personal merit (Romans 3:10-12, 23), that God's standard of righteousness cannot be achieved by any human good works (Ephesians 2:8-9), that everything in his life is secondary to following Christ (Matthew 10:37; Mark 10:21; Luke 9:23), and that Jesus is God in the flesh (John 1:14; Philippians 2:5-11) and Lord of all (Matthew 7:21-23; 28:18), willing and able to save through His sacrificial death on the cross (1 Peter 2:24). The application of the gospel through the effective call of God results in:

repentance (Acts 2:38; 11:18); faith in Christ (Galatians 2:16; Ephesians 2:8-9); calling on the Lord (Romans 10:14); verbal confession of Christ (Romans 10:10); and a changed life (Luke 19:8; 1 John 2:4). The message of the gospel is foolishness to the unsaved because it assaults man's wisdom (1 Corinthians 1:18, 24), and yet it is the only power that can save (Romans 1:16).

We deny that the gospel is dependent on the wisdom and cleverness of man. We deny that the gospel is social action, mere "belief in Jesus", love, faith in faith, acts of mercy, or any "supernatural" event apart from what is revealed in the Bible. We deny that any message that excludes repentance of sin, belief in the person and work of Christ on the cross, the lordship of Christ and coming to Christ by faith, is the gospel. We deny that the gospel is mediated through any non-scriptural decree, church, priest, religious activity, icon, or artifact.

8.5 The Atonement - We believe the Scriptures teach that the work of Jesus on the cross made atonement for the sins of the elect (Romans 8:32-33). Scripture is clear that the atonement is applied to "His people" (Matthew 1:21), His own sheep (John 10:15), those given to Him by the Father (John 6:37; 44), and those who make up the church (Acts 20:28; Ephesians 5:25). In Jesus' high priestly prayer in John 17:9, He does not intercede on behalf of everyone in the world but only for those given to Him by the Father. Atonement refers to the covering of sin through the death of Christ that did not merely make man savable, or merely able to be saved, but, in fact, did everything necessary to save him. Atonement includes the completed work of reconciliation (Romans 5:10; Ephesians 2:14-16), propitiation (1 John 4:10), and eternal redemption (Hebrews 9:12). These are finished works which do not ultimately depend on the choice of mankind to be implemented. It is incorrect to think that Jesus' death paid for the sins of every person in the world, as some interpret 1 John 2:2. That would either result in universalism or a double payment for sin, once by Jesus on the cross, and the other by the condemned sinner in hell (Romans 6:23). Jesus' covering for the sins of the "whole world" (1 John 2:2) is best understood in His gathering His own sheep from "out of the world" (John 11:52; 13:1; Revelation 5:9).

We deny that the atonement did not purchase a specific people and simply provided the way for man to be saved thus making the atonement ineffective and completely dependent on the choice or work of man. We deny universal or potential atonement.

8.6 Propitiation - We believe the Scriptures teach that the symbolism of the Old Testament mercy seat where the blood of the sacrificial lamb was sprinkled (Leviticus 16:14-16; Hebrews 9:25), offers a picture of propitiation that refers to the appeasing of the wrath of God by the offering of a sufficient sacrifice for sin. This is an eternal, unchangeable requirement of a holy and just God regarding the sins of mankind that necessitated an eternal, unchangeable solution for sin (2 Corinthians 5:21; Hebrews 9:11-14). Jesus' sacrificial death covers the sins of those who repent (1 Peter 3:18; 2 Peter 3:9). Religious ritual and the efforts of man cannot satisfy God (Hebrews 10:4, 11). In order for Christ to be a high priest for man He had to be made like man so that He could satisfy man's need for identification with Him, as well as the Father's need for justice (Hebrews 2:17). This public display of Jesus on the cross demonstrated God's satisfaction with Jesus' sacrifice, passing over the sins of the redeemed in order to show His righteousness by justifying them (Romans 3:25-26).

We deny that God was not satisfied with the death of Christ. We deny that God is looking for anything in addition to the finished work on the cross to bring about salvation.

8.7 Justification – We believe the Scriptures teach that justification is a legal action in which God declares those who, through faith in Christ, have repented of their sins (Matthew 3:8; Acts 2:38; Romans 2:4), and confessed Christ as their sovereign Lord (Romans 10:9-10; 1 Corinthians 12:3), to be freed from sin and made righteous because of the imputation of their sins to Christ (Romans 6:18; Colossians 2:14;1 Peter 2:24), and the imputation of His righteousness to them (Romans 4:5; 5:1; 2 Corinthians 5:21). Since justification is a legal pardon for sin, this means that God treats all those who receive His gift of eternal life by faith as completely justified under the law, entitled to all the privileges due those, hypothetically, who have perfectly kept the law (Romans 3:26, 28; 4:16). This frees the recipient from all condemnation, not because he has changed his behavior, though he will, but because God now views him as being guilt-free (Romans 8:1, 33-34).

We deny that man can be made right with God through adherence to any Pope, church, priest, person, council, creed, religious tradition, or any good work. We deny that the righteousness of God is earned or deserved in any way, or is imputed to the believer through anything other than faith. We deny as biblical justification any teaching that distorts, confuses, or contradicts the doctrine of salvation through grace alone, by faith alone, in Christ alone.

8.8 Sanctification – We believe the Scriptures teach that every believer is declared holy through justification and made holy through sanctification. Believers are identified as saints positionally, having nothing to do with the believer's present walk or condition (Acts 20:32; 1 Corinthians 1:2; 2 Thessalonians 2:13; Hebrews 10:14). But we also teach that the Bible indicates a progressive sanctification through which the believer is conformed to the image of Christ over time (Romans 8:28-30). The life of the believer is a daily struggle against sin which still indwells his flesh (Romans 7:18-19). To say that one has conquered all sin is untrue and unbiblical (Philippians 3:12; 1 John 1:8, 10; 2:1). But the believer, acting with the cooperation of the Holy Spirit, mortifies fleshly desires, and empowers the activities of the new nature in consecration to God (Romans 6:4-6, 13, 16; 8:13; Galatians 2:19; 5:24; Colossians 2:2-3; 3:1-2) so that the believer does not practice sin as a way of life (1 John 3:5-10). Sanctification occurs as the believer receives instruction from the Word and is continually washed and cleansed by it (Psalm 119:105; John 17:17; Ephesians 5:26). As the Word sanctifies, the believer is more desirous of following the Holy Spirit's leading (Romans 12:1-2; 2 Corinthians 3:18; Ephesians 4:24; Philippians 1:6; 1 Thessalonians 5:23). The bottom line is that genuine Christianity will manifest itself outwardly in the life of the believer (John 13:35; Romans 5:3-5; James 2:14, 26; 2 Peter 1:8-11) in spiritual endurance (2 Timothy 2:12), good works (Ephesians 2:10; James 2:17-18), spiritual fruit (Matthew 7:15-20), and a life of faith that will "adorn the doctrine of God our Savior in every respect" (Titus 2:10).

We deny any claim of sinless perfectionism. But we also deny that a Christian will continue to practice sin as a way of life without a conviction of sin. We also deny the ability of any form of modern psychology to bring about biblical sanctification.

8.9 Perseverance – Salvation is completely the work of God (John 3:16-18; Romans 5:6; 1 Timothy 4:10), yet the believer is one who perseveres to the end (John 8:31-32; Romans 8:22-23; 1 Corinthians 1:8-9; Colossians 1:22-23; 1 Peter 1:4-5; Jude 24). This means that the character of a Christian's life will prove that he is a Christian (Galatians 5:22-23; 1 John 2:3-11). Though the believer's life will give evidence that he is saved, he will not live a perfect life (1 John 1:8). The certainty of man's salvation lays in the faithfulness of God (John 10:28-29; Romans 11:29; 2 Timothy 1:12; 4:18). When God grants eternal life, Christians respond by practicing Spirit-filled qualities of living, which confirms God's calling and choosing in their lives (2 Peter 1:4-11). True believers are not saved through perseverance but demonstrate their calling and election and that they are children of God because they will persevere (Matthew 10:22; 24:13; Hebrews 10:36; 1 John 2:19; Revelation 2:26).

We deny that a true Christian can lose his salvation or renounce his faith. We deny sinless perfectionism and pharisaic legalism.

8.10 Glorification - We believe that "glorification" is the final phase in the divine process of God's redemptive plan in Christ. We believe that it is impossible for those whom God has foreknown, predestined, called and justified by Christ's person and cross-work to ever slip out of the life-giving process of God's salvation without also finally being glorified. (Romans 8: 28-30). We believe that since Christ alone is our true hope, not only will we someday be with the Lord himself, but we are also going to be just like him (Matthew 13:43; 1 John 3:2; Colossians 3:4; Philippians 3:20-21). Scripture indicates that Jesus was raised in the same body in which he died, and we believe this will also be the case with all true believers; raised up in the same physical organism but naturally different. (1 Corinthians 15:42-44). We believe that the final state in glorification would be a raising up of the physical body into an imperishable and immortal state. (1 Corinthians 15:51-53). We believe that the believer's glorified body will be like Christ's, impervious to death and sickness, with spirit and soul filled to the brim with righteousness and truth. The grief and burdens that the temporal life can bring will trouble us no longer. Even the very presence of sin will be eradicated, and the "sanctification" process will be completed. We believe that all true believers (dead and alive) from the church age will go through this marvelous, sudden and supernatural transformation which will take place at the return of The Lord Jesus to catch away or "rapture" His church. (John 14:3; 1 Thessalonians 4:13-17).

ARTICLE NINE
The Church

9.1 The Universal Church - We believe the Scriptures teach that all people who embrace the gospel of Jesus Christ through repentance, faith and confession are immediately placed into His body, the church, by the Holy Spirit (1 Corinthians 12:12-13). This is one body, comprised of believers from every nation, tribe, and people (Revelation 5:9; 7:9) whose head is Christ Himself (Romans 12:5; 1 Corinthians12:12-13; Ephesians 1:22; Colossians 1:18). The church was formed as a visible body on the day of Pentecost (Acts 2:1-21, 38-47) and will complete her earthly work at the rapture of the church (John14:1-4; 1 Corinthians 15:51-52; 1 Thessalonians 4:13-18). Because God has called each individual member of the church (Romans 1:6; 8:28; 1 Corinthians 1:24; Revelation 17:14), the corporate assembly of called ones is referred to as a "chosen race, a royal priesthood, a holy nation, a people for God's own possession" (1 Peter 2:9). The church is also distinct from Israel in God's historical timetable. When the "time of the Gentiles" (Luke 21:24) is completed at the end of the seven-year tribulation (Daniel 9:24-27), God will fulfill all of His promises of restoration to a literal, earthly nation of Israel who will recognize Jesus as their Messiah and turn to Him in repentance (Zechariah 12:10) during a literal earthly kingdom that will last for a thousand years (Revelation 20:4-6).

We deny that the universal invisible church makes the local visible church unnecessary. We deny that any one church organization or denomination, including the Roman Catholic Church, is the true church. We deny that anyone old enough to perceive the gospel can be a part of the true church without repenting of their sin and confessing Christ as Lord and Savior.

9.2 The Local Church - We believe the Scriptures teach that God's pattern for evangelism, discipleship, worship, missions, and ministry takes place in the context of the local church (Matthew 28:19-20; Acts 13:1; 14:26-27; Ephesians 4:11-12). The effectiveness of a local church is seen in faithful preaching (1 Corinthians 1:21), God-honoring worship (Mark 12:30), obedient evangelism (Romans 10:14), biblical discipleship (Romans 15:14; 1 Thessalonians 5:14), and biblical ministry (Ephesians 4:11-12). The characteristics of a local church are the headship of Christ (Colossians 1:18), the leadership of male elders (Acts 14:23; 1 Timothy 3:1-7; Titus 1:5), the service of deacons and deaconesses (Acts 6:1-6;1 Timothy 3:8-13), regular meetings (Hebrews 10:25), financial giving to meet the needs of the body (2 Corinthians 8-9), orderly corporate worship centered on the exposition of the Word of God (1 Corinthians 14:25-40), Biblical fellowship (1 John 1:3, 7), constant prayer (1 Thessalonians 5:17), believer's baptism (Matthew 28:19-20; Acts 2:38; 8:12-16; 10:47), the regular observance of the Lord's Supper (1 Corinthians 11:23-34), the exercise of church discipline (Matthew 18:15-18), and the exercise of spiritual gifts that builds the body up and ministers to their needs (1 Corinthians 12:4-11, 28-31; Ephesians 4:11-12). Each local body yields spiritual authority to its leaders (Matthew 18:17; Hebrews 13:17), is known for their love (John 13:35), carries on the work of ministry as they are equipped by godly pastors (Ephesians 4:11-12), and are willing to suffer for the name of Jesus (1 Thessalonians 2:14; 1 Peter 4:12-19).

We deny that any Christian can truly follow Christ unless he has a love for His bride (the Church) and manifests that love through faithful involvement with a visible, local church if one is available. We deny that a biblical church can build a biblical ministry based on psychology, pragmatism, marketing techniques, cultural trends, mass media communication tools, or a post-modern worldview that diminishes the role of doctrinal propositions or the value of gathering as a church.

9.3 The Ordinances of the Church - We believe the Scriptures teach that baptism and the Lord's Table are ordained as memorials in the Bible, but they do not save.

Baptism - We believe the Scriptures teach that water baptism is not a personal choice but that every true disciple of Christ is to be baptized as an initial act of obedience (Matthew 28:19-20; Acts 2:38; 16:33; 19:5), as a picture of the death, burial, and resurrection of Jesus Christ (Romans 6:3-5), and as a public act of identification (Matthew 10:32-33; Romans 6:3). We believe the Scriptures teach that baptism of a believer by immersion is the command and practice of Scripture (Matthew 28:19-20; Acts 2:38-39). Scripture points to believers in each case where baptism is observed (Acts 2:38-39; 8:38; 9:18), even in the "household" passages often used, erroneously, to give support for infant baptism (Acts 10:2; 16:34; 18:8; 1 Corinthians 1:14). Thus, nothing in Scripture indicates we are to baptize infants. Immersion is indicated by the selection of the word baptidzo, which means "to immerse, sink, or drown", and thus is the practice of the New Testament (Matthew 3:16; Acts 8:38).

The Lord's Table - We believe the Scriptures teach the second ordinance to be observed by the church is the Lord's Table (Communion) (1 Corinthians 11:23-26). The Lord's Table is to be observed only by believers who have made every attempt to be in right-standing with God and man (Matthew 5:23-24; 1 Corinthians 11:27-29). It symbolizes Christ's atoning sacrifice for sin (1 Corinthians 11:25-26), spiritual nourishment (John 6:53-57), the unity believers have in Him (1 Corinthians 10:17), the joy of His return (Luke 22:18; 1 Corinthians 11:26), and the purity of the body of Christ (John 6:56; 1 Corinthians 11:27-29).The bread represents the body of Christ and the cup represents the blood of Christ in a symbolic representation of the New Covenant, which is based on the shed blood of Christ as the covering for sin (Jeremiah 31:31-34; Ephesians 1:7; Hebrews 9:22). The Lord's Table is a literal fulfillment of the New Covenant promised in (Jeremiah 31:31-34) which promised salvation to all who know the God of Israel as revealed in Jesus Christ (Matthew 26:28).

We deny that baptism other than one performed after a person has placed their personal faith in Christ is Biblical. We deny that baptism is the beginning of regeneration. We deny that any form of baptism other than that of immersion is the Biblical norm. We deny that the bread and cup are in any way the literal body of Christ. This is affirmed by the fact that he was standing in front of the disciples in His physical body as He spoke the words "my body and my blood" and administered the first Lord's Table. We deny that the Lord's Table and baptism are sacraments in the Roman Catholic sense of being signs or means of man's justification. But we also deny that they are mere options for believers.

9.4 Church Membership - We believe the Scriptures teach that the New Testament church knew how many people were in their churches and who they were (Acts 1:15; 2:41, 4:4, 35; Romans 16:3-16). There are solid Biblical indicators of local church membership. These include keeping track of those new converts added "to their number" (Acts 2:41, 47; 5:14), the keeping of a list of names of widows to be fed and put on a list for financial aid (Acts 6:1; 1 Timothy 5:9), letters of commendation written when people moved (Acts 18:27; Romans 16:1; 2 Corinthians 3:1-2; Colossians 4:10), and terms used which suggest well-defined boundaries of church membership (Acts 6:5; 8:1; 9:26; 14:23; 15:17; 20:17; 1 Corinthians 5:4). Membership reflects a visible manifestation of the invisible church (Romans 12:5; 1 Corinthians 12:13), submission to authority (Matthew 18:18-20; Hebrews 13:17), mutual commitment (Romans 12:10), a desire to serve (Ephesians 4:12), a purpose for living (Ephesians 1:11), and unity in the body (Ephesians 4:3-6). Practically, membership allows the elders of the church to know the ones under their care who have made a public commitment to Christ and ascribe to the values of the church, provides a screening for leadership positions, and presents a visible, unified body to the community.

We deny that a commitment of membership to a local church is optional. We deny that being involved in multiple churches for different activities is the biblical pattern of commitment to the body of Christ.

9.5 Church Government – We believe the Scriptures teach that the local church is to be self-governing (Matthew 18:20; Acts 14:23; 1 Thessalonians 5:12, 27; Titus 1:5; 1 Peter 2:9) and ruled by a plurality of godly male elders (Acts 14:23; Titus 1:5). All of the qualities for church overseers are applied to men (1 Timothy 3:1-7; Titus 1:5-9), and the Bible specifically states that women are not to teach or have authority over men (1 Timothy 2:12). Elders are appointed for their godly character and gifts of leadership (1 Timothy 3:1-7; Titus 1:5-9), and must be fully accountable to God's Word as they lead their local church. They are not accountable to any outside earthly or religious authority in issues of doctrine and practice (Daniel 6:4-13; Acts 4:19; 5:29). This does not rule out a leader among leaders as seen in the ministry of Paul (Philippians 3:17; 4:9), Timothy (2 Timothy 1:6; 2:2), Titus (Titus 1:5), and James (Acts 15:13, 19). Though describing different functions, the words pastor, elder, and overseer are synonymous (Acts 20:17, 28; 1 Peter 5:1-2) and are the only ones used to describe those in leadership in the local church. Some have the role and gift of preaching and teaching the flock (1 Timothy 4:6, 11-16; 2 Timothy 4:2), while some are given more to ruling or oversight (1 Timothy 5:17). Elders are also to equip the flock to do the work of ministry (Ephesians 4:11-12), serve as doctrinal guardians for the church (1 Timothy 1:10; 4:6; 6:3; 2 Timothy 2:24-25; Titus 1:9), and provide pastoral oversight and shepherding for the entire church (1 Peter 5:1-3). Deacons and deaconesses are spiritually qualified men and women who minister to the practical needs of the church under the oversight of the elders (Acts 6:3; 1 Timothy 3:8-13). The congregation is to respond with loving appreciation and obedience to those in these leadership positions (1 Thessalonians 5:12-13; Hebrews 13:17).

We deny that the roles of men and women in the Bible are culturally conditioned or the results of an oppressive patriarchal society. We deny that the biblical restriction on women in church leadership inhibits their meaningful role as ministers in the church, teachers of women and children or mentors and models for younger women. We deny the authority of any spiritual leader outside the local church. We deny the biblical validity of a purely congregational or episcopal form of government.

9.6 Evangelism – Since the identity of the elect is unknown to man, the responsibility of individual Christians is to share the gospel at every opportunity (Matthew 28:19-20; Acts 1:8; 13:47-48; 2 Timothy 2:10). This is an individual calling (1 Corinthians 9:19-23; 2 Timothy 4:5), though God also uses the preaching of the Word in the church to bring conviction to the unsaved (1 Corinthians 14:24-25). Christians are to be ready and able to make a presentation of the gospel (1 Peter 3:15), live it out in the context of their lives (Acts 2:47), and implore others to be reconciled to Christ (2 Corinthians 5:18-20). In addition, Christians are to go to those who don't know about Christ and preach to them so that they can hear, believe, and call upon the name of the Lord (Romans 10:14-15). Believers are to evangelize knowing that the power and success of the gospel is predicated on the work of the Holy Spirit, not the clever devices and persuasive speech of man (Romans 1:16; 8:28-30). They are not to be ashamed to proclaim the gospel, realizing that a clear and accurate presentation alone has power to bring conversion and add people to the Kingdom as God chooses (Acts 2:47; 13:48; Romans 1:16).

We deny that the doctrine of election precludes the need for evangelism. We deny that evangelism can be reduced to a person, program, event, technique, or marketing approach. We deny the biblical nature of evangelistic methods that exclude sin, repentance, the cross, the resurrection, faith, and the Lordship of Christ. We deny that the "wideness of God's mercy" extends saving grace to sincere people of other faiths who do not confess Christ as Lord and Savior.

ARTICLE TEN
Eschatology (End Times)

10.1 The Rapture – We believe the Scriptures teach that at death the spirit and soul of the believer passes instantly into the presence of Christ and remains in conscious joy until the resurrection of the body when Christ comes for his own (2 Corinthians 5:8; 1 Corinthians 15:51-57). We believe the Scriptures teach the Lord will return at an unknown time in the future to catch away (rapture) the church from the earth to meet Him in the air (John 14:3; 1 Thessalonians 4:13-17). This could happen at any time since no one knows the timing of the return of Christ except the Father (1 Corinthians 15:51-52; 1 Thessalonians 1:10). The Raptureis a comforting event and a "blessed hope" for Christians since it assures them of the return of Christ and His preparation of a place for them in heaven (John 14:3, 1 Thessalonians 4:18; Titus 2:13). Although there are three major views of the timing of the Rapture, some placing it at the beginning, some in the middle, and some at the end of the seven-year Tribulation, we believe the Scriptures teach that the Rapture will occur prior to the great Tribulation and also prior to the millennial reign of Christ.

We deny that the Rapture is to be interpreted allegorically, or that it is a secret event, or that it is partial in nature. We deny that the Rapture should be spiritualized in any way. We deny that the Rapture and the Second Coming of Christ are the same event.

10.2 The Tribulation - We believe the Scriptures teach that the Tribulation is a seven-year period of time which will precede the Second Coming of Christ (Matthew 24:3-31; Revelation 6:1-18:24). This period is the 70th week of Daniel (Daniel 9:24-27) and is marked by the unleashed wrath of God against the unsaved wicked on the earth who continue to live in a defiant, unrepentant state (Isaiah 26:20-21; Jeremiah 30:7; Joel 1:15; 1 Thessalonians 1:9-10; Revelation 6:16-17; 9:21; 16:1). It will be a demonstration of the wrath of God such as the world has never seen before (Isaiah 24:1-5; Matthew 24:15-21). But it will also be a time of continuous evangelistic work and harvest (Revelation 6:9; 7:3, 9, 14; 11:3; 12:10-11; 14:6).

We deny that the Tribulation should be interpreted allegorically or that we are now living through the events described in Revelation 6-19. We also deny that these events occurred before 70 AD.

10.3 The Second Coming - We believe the Scriptures teach that Jesus Christ will return physically to the earth (Matthew 24:29-31; Revelation 19:11-21, 20:4-5;) when His feet touch down on the Mount of Olives (Zechariah 14:3-4) at the end of the Tribulation. He will defeat Antichrist (Revelation 19:11-21) and all the nations that rise against Israel (Zechariah 14:4-5; 2 Thessalonians 1:7-10). His coming will inaugurate a literal thousand-year millennial kingdom (Zechariah 14:9-21; Matthew 25:31; Revelation 20:4) and Satan will be bound and cast into the abyss for a thousand years (Revelation 20:2-3).

We deny that the Rapture is the same event as the Second Coming of Jesus Christ.

10.4 The Millennium - We believe the Scriptures teach that immediately after the Second Coming of Christ, Jesus will begin a literal thousand-year reign on the earth (Revelation 20:1-6). During this time He will rule as king (Isaiah 9:3-7; 11:1-10) in Jerusalem as the capital of the world (Zechariah 8:3-8). The nation of Israel will receive all the spiritual and physical blessings promised her as she is restored to her promised land (Isaiah 11:10-12; Ezekiel 37:21-28), having turned to her Messiah (Micah 7:18-19; Zephaniah 13:1; Zechariah 12:10-14; Romans 11:26-27) and embraced Him in faith. This will be a time of peace (Isaiah 32:17-18; Micah 4:2-4), joy (Isaiah 61:7, 10), and comfort (Isaiah 40:1-2), with no poverty (Amos 9:13-15) or sickness (Isaiah 35:5-6). Unbelieving Gentile nations will be judged in the Valley of Jehoshaphat (the Kidron Valley) immediately following the Second Coming of Christ, (Joel 3:2, 12), probably during the extra 75 days at the end of the Tribulation mentioned by Daniel (Daniel 12:11-12). Even though only believers will enter the millennial kingdom (Revelation 19:21), they will still be subjected to their fleshly desires (Revelation 20:4). Despite the blessings of the millennial kingdom, some who are born during this time will reject Christ. At the end of the Millennium, Satan will again be released to deceive the nations and attempt to lead them in a battle against God (Revelation 20:3, 7). But God will immediately devour them with fire coming down from heaven and Satan and all who follow him will be thrown into the Lake of Fire forever (Revelation 20:9-10). Following this, God will judge all unbelievers at the Great White Throne Judgment and all whose names are not found in the Book of Life will also be thrown into the Lake of Fire to receive their punishment forever (Revelation 20:11-15). Jesus will then deliver up the kingdom to the Father having put all things in subjection under His feet (1 Corinthians 15:24-28).The eternal state will then be ushered in, along with a new heaven and a new earth, and there shall no longer be any mourning or crying or pain (2 Peter 3:10-12; Revelation 21:1-22:7).

We deny that God has replaced Israel with the Church, and that there is no future for the nation of Israel in prophecy. We deny that the Rapture, the Millennium, and the Second Coming of Christ occurred in the first century.

10.5 Heaven - We believe the Scriptures teach that heaven is an actual place, prepared by Christ for the glory and enjoyment of the redeemed of all time forever and ever (Romans 8:21; Revelation 22:5). All believers will enter into a new heaven and new earth immediately after the Great White Throne Judgment (Revelation 21:1), when the present heavens and earth will be destroyed in divine judgment (2 Peter 3:10, 13; Revelation 20:11). In the place of the first heaven and earth, God will create a new heaven and new earth where the corruption of the first heaven and earth will not be remembered and the things to come will remain forever (Isaiah 65:17; 66:22). Christians look forward to this new heaven with great joy since it is the place ruled by righteousness because Jesus Himself dwells and rules there (Revelation 21:22-23). A completely new Jerusalem will come down out of heaven and become the residence of the redeemed forever (Revelation 21:2). There will be no sea in the new Jerusalem, indicative of a whole new metaphysical existence (Revelation 21:1).There will also be no death, mourning, weeping, or pain in heaven (Revelation 21:4). In addition, the curse pronounced in the Garden of Eden will be removed (Revelation 22:3), and night itself will cease to exist since Jesus Himself is the light of heaven (Revelation 21:25; 22:5). God Himself will reside with His people (Revelation 21:3) and the redeemed will experience a perfect relationship with Him in recognizable, glorified bodies (John 20:16-17; 1 Corinthians 15:4-8), transformed and fit for heaven by His creative power (1 Corinthians 15:49, 51; Philippians 3:21). This will enable believers to enjoy the exquisite physical and spiritual perfections of heaven where gold and precious jewels will be common building materials (Revelation 21:18-21), abundant vegetation will enrich their lives (Revelation 22:2), and their existence will be marked by praise, unity, communion, and perfect harmony forever (Revelation 22:5).

We deny that heaven is a myth concocted by man to make himself feel better about dying. We deny that heaven is merely spiritual, existing only in man's mind and aspirations. We deny that heaven is the eventual destiny of all people.

10.6 Hell – We believe the Scriptures teach that all whose names are not in the Book of Life will be resurrected and sentenced to the Lake of Fire to be tormented forever (Revelation 20:12). The fact that the Antichrist and the false prophet, who were condemned to the Lake of Fire at the beginning of the millennium (Revelation 19:20) and are still there one thousand years later (Revelation 20:10) repudiates the concept of annihilation. Those in hell will experience never-ending conscious agony, both physically and emotionally. This is seen in the picture of unquenchable fire (judgment) (Matthew 3:12), outer darkness (separation) (Matthew 8:12; 22:13; 25:30), weeping (great sadness and emotional anguish) (Matthew 8:12; 13:42; 13:50; 22:13; 25:30); the "gnashing of teeth," (extreme hate or anger) (Matthew 8:12; 13:42; 22:13; 25:30), and never-ending emotional torment (Matthew 25:46; Luke 16:23, 28; Revelation 14:11; 20:10). All who go to hell go there because they reject natural revelation (Romans 1:20), deny their own conscience (Romans 2:14-16), desire to live their own lives separate from God (Philippians 3:18-19), and their deeds deserve it (Revelation 20:12). They will be thrown into hell by God (John 15:16; Revelation 20:15) to be punished for their sin against God forever (Matthew 25:46; Hebrews 10:29).

We deny that hell is here on earth. We deny that unbelievers will simply be annihilated after death or at any time in the future. We deny the existence of purgatory or that there will be a "second chance" for those in hell or that the punishment will expire after a certain time.

ARTICLE ELEVEN
Christian Living

We believe that the Scriptures teach that a Christian should live for the glory of God and the well-being of his fellow men; that his conduct should be blameless before the world; that he should be a faithful steward of his time and possessions; and that he should seek for himself and others the full stature of maturity in Christ. The Christian life should be one of faith expressing itself through love and is lived through the power of the Holy Spirit and not through the observance of the law or any rules of men. A true believer's life should be characterized by the increasing display of the Spirit's control and by the fruit of the Spirit and also by prayer, a love for the Bible, and an attitude of humility, submission and forgiveness.

1 Cor. 10:31; Rom. 12:1-3; Heb. 12:1-2; John 14:15, 23-24; 1 John 2:3-6; 2 Cor. 9:6-9; 1 Cor. 4:2; Col. 1:9-10; Gal. 5:5-16, 22-26; Eph. 4:32

TEACHER AFFIRMATION

I have read and understand the above Doctrinal Teaching Statement which expresses the Biblical doctrines as held by Valley Bible Church. As one who desires to teach at Valley Bible Church, I agree not to advocate a position that would be contrary to any of the elements in this doctrinal teaching statement.

☐ Yes ☐ No

Print Name: ______________________________ Date: ____________

Sign: ____________________________________

www.ingramcontent.com/pod-product-compliance
Ingram Content Group UK Ltd.
Pitfield, Milton Keynes, MK11 3LW, UK
UKHW022008190726
13853UKWH00004B/1805

9 798473 989328